UMOREN KOKO

Romans 14:17 – KJV
For the kingdom of God is not meat and drink; but righteousness, and peace, and joy in the Holy Ghost.

RIGHTEOUSNESS, PEACE, & JOY.

UMOREN KOKO

ISBN   978-978-59058-9-2

Published in Nigeria by
WIND CHILD

Copyright © Umoren Koko 2023

All scriptures are taken from the King James Version of the Bible. This version was preferred because it is an earlier version than most of the other versions of the Bible in circulation.

Many other versions are basically interpretations and translations of the KJV. Therefore, to avoid this work being influenced by a third party's interpretation or translation, the KJV became the preferred Bible.

CONTENTS

DEDICATION

This book is dedicated to you the reader.

INTRODUCTION

Mental health issues have become common place in this generation. It is so frightening to see the rate of suicide amongst young people, old people, rich people, poor people, and all people in general. This is proof of the lack of joy that is abundant in this era. Further proof of the lack of joy is the high rate of crime, wars, sexually transmitted diseases, and other negative parameters affecting society. Although, it can be argued that the aforementioned parameters like crime and others are more causes than symptoms of the lack of Joy in society.

Something that calls out for my attention is that majority of the symptoms or causes of this prevalent lack of joy are more predominant in highly religious societies. Whether it's high crime rate, STDs, poverty, and many more, these things seem to be more present, the more religious a society is. Being born as a Christian and growing up as a Christian, I hope it would be seen as an admission rather than an accusation when I point out that most of these negative things are more prevalent in Christian societies.

Why is this the case? What have we gotten wrong that has led us to this point where Joy is a very scarce commodity?

How are we going to find Joy?

To answer this question, one passage in the bible comes to mind.

Romans 14:17 - KJV

17. For the kingdom of God is not meat and drink; but righteousness, and peace, and joy in the Holy Ghost.

This passage says that Joy is part of the kingdom of God which is in the holy ghost.

This is a strange one because the majority of Christians speak about the holy ghost as a very familiar entity. One that many preachers claim to be friends with. Yet why then is Joy such an unfamiliar experience?

Maybe the problem is in the kingdom of God. Many Christians believe that the kingdom of God is a place where God is and where we go when we die as Christians. If this is the case, then that might explain the scarcity of Joy. Perhaps we need to die and go to the kingdom of God before we can experience Joy. But if that is the case then it means we should just give up on the concept of Joy. But this conclusion comes with one very important question; if we can only get to the kingdom of God after we die, does this mean that we can only experience righteousness, peace, and joy after we die, then we can only access the holly Ghost after we die because according to Romans 14:17, righteousness, Peace, and Joy are in the kingdom of God and also in the Holly Ghost at the same time?

If this is the case then we need to question all those who claim to have a relationship with the holy ghost.

This definitely can't be the case because according to the bible, many people have worked with and by the holy ghost.

Mark 12:36 – KJV

36.   For David himself said by the **Holy Ghost,** *The LORD said to my Lord, Sit thou on my right hand, till I make thine enemies thy footstool.*

Mark 13:11 – KJV

11.   But when they shall lead you, and deliver you up, take no thought beforehand what ye shall speak, neither do ye premeditate: but whatsoever shall be given you in that hour, that speak ye: for it is not ye that speak, but the **Holy Ghost.**

2 Peter 1:21 - KJV

21.   For the prophecy came not in old time by the will of man: but holy men of God spake as they were moved by the **Holy Ghost.**

So, it is possible to function with the holy ghost while you are alive therefore you can experience Joy while you are alive. Thus, you should be able to access the kingdom of God while you are alive.

This means for us to understand how to experience Joy, we would need to understand two key concepts of Christianity, namely the kingdom of God and the holy ghost.

15

THE KINGDOM OF GOD

The kingdom of God is the centre of the gospel preached by Jesus. While many people still debate about the ministry of Jesus and why he was sent, there is only one place in the bible where he clearly states what his assignment and mission is.

Luke 4:43 - KJV

43.   And he said unto them, I must preach the kingdom of God to other cities also: for therefore am I sent.

But before we proceed in this chapter, I would like to let you take note that there is no difference between the kingdom of God and the kingdom of heaven. The only thing is that in the book of Mathew, the kingdom of heaven is used while the other three gospels make use of the kingdom of God to mean the same thing. This is evident in the fact that the same story that is told in Mathew would say the kingdom of heaven while the other gospels would say the kingdom of God while narrating the same story.

Matthew 4:17 - KJV

17.   From that time Jesus began to preach, and to say, Repent: for the **kingdom of heaven** is at hand.

Mark 1:14-15 - KJV

14.   Now after that John was put in prison, Jesus came into Galilee, preaching the gospel of the **kingdom of God,**

15.   And saying, The time is fulfilled, and the **kingdom of God** is at hand: repent ye, and believe the gospel.

The verses above, do not only show that the kingdom of God and the kingdom of heaven are used interchangeably, but they also show the gospel preached by Jesus. However, the dispute or the confusion about the gospel of Jesus comes mostly from Luke 17:21.

Luke 17:20-21 - KJV

20.   And when he was demanded of the Pharisees, when the kingdom of God should come, he answered them and said, The kingdom of God cometh not with observation:

21.   Neither shall they say, Lo here! or, lo there! for, behold, the **kingdom of God is within you.**

The problem or confusion here is that Jesus said that the kingdom of God was inside a person. This has led to a big argument about the kingdom of God. Many Christians believe that the kingdom of God is a place where true Christians go after they die. But some other Christians and theologians argue that it is not a place. I am on the side of the latter. I believe that those who think that Jesus was talking about a place are wrong and are flirting with ignorance.

If you look at the gospel preached by Jesus in Matthew 4:17 and Mark 1:14-15, you would observe that Jesus also says that the kingdom of God is at hand. If you say something is at hand, you mean that the thing is in one's possession. To put it literally, you are saying that the person has it in his/her hands. This correlates with the statement that the kingdom of God is within You. If the kingdom of God was a place, how can it be within a person and how can it be in someone's hands or possession?

The answer is simple, the kingdom of God that Jesus was talking about isn't a place. If the kingdom of God isn't a place, then what is it?

After asking God this same question for a long time, I got my answer one morning in the most unlikely of manners. God simply reminded me of my biology class in secondary school. When living organisms were divided based on their character and nature, they were divided into kingdoms. According to biologists, the five kingdom categories of living organisms are Protista (the single-celled eukaryotes); Fungi

(fungus and related organisms); Plantae (the plants); Animalia (the animals); Monera (the prokaryotes). This means the word kingdom could have been used to describe
characteristics or way of life or nature at some time in history.

I decided to put this interpretation into the bible and then I finally got the understanding I was looking for. If the word kingdom means characteristics/way of life/nature, then let us use this new understanding to interpret the teachings of Jesus and see if they explain things better.

Matthew 6:33 - KJV

33. But seek ye first the **kingdom of God,** *and his righteousness; and all these things shall be added unto you.*

This verse could mean, seek ye first the character/nature/way of life of God; and all these things shall be added unto you.

Luke 4:43 - KJV

43. And he said unto them, I must preach the kingdom of God to other cities also: for therefore am I sent.

This verse therefore means I must preach the character/way of life/ behaviour of God to other cities also: for therefore am I sent.

Matthew 4:17 - KJV

17.   From that time Jesus began to preach, and to say, Repent: for the kingdom of heaven is at hand.

Mark 1:14-15 - KJV

14.   Now after that John was put in prison, Jesus came into Galilee, preaching the gospel of the kingdom of God,

15.   And saying, The time is fulfilled, and the **kingdom of God is at hand:** *repent ye, and believe the gospel.*

These verses will therefore mean that Jesus was saying repent for the nature/character/way of life/behaviour of God is in your possession. This begins to make a lot of sense when you consider Luke 10:20-21.

Luke 17:20-21 - KJV

20.   And when he was demanded of the Pharisees, when the kingdom of God should come, he answered them and said, The kingdom of God cometh not with observation:

*21.   Neither shall they say, Lo here! or, lo there! for, behold, **the kingdom of God is within you**.*

These verses mean that Jesus was saying that the nature/character/way of life/behaviour of God is within you. This also gets interesting when you observe that Jesus wasn't even talking to his disciples in this verse, he was talking to Pharisees. How could he have told the Pharisees that the kingdom of God was within them?

This is simply because the kingdom of God is not a place. Things begin to make sense when you take this understanding into our key text for this book Roman 14:17.

Romans 14:17 - KJV

17.   For the kingdom of God is not meat and drink; but righteousness, and peace, and joy in the Holy Ghost.

This verse will therefore mean that the nature of God is not in meat and drink; but in righteousness, peace, and joy. Another way to put it is that living like God means that you would be expressing these three things; righteousness, peace, and joy.

THE HOLY GHOST

Romans 14:17 - KJV

17.   For the kingdom of God is not meat and drink; but righteousness, and peace, and joy **in the Holy Ghost.**

Luke 17:21 - KJV

21. Neither shall they say, Lo here! or, lo there! for, behold, the kingdom of God **is within you.**

Mark 1:15 - KJV

15.   And saying, The time is fulfilled, and the kingdom of God **is at hand:** *repent ye, and believe the gospel.*

The kingdom of God according to Jesus, is within you or in other words, it is at hand. But according to the writer of the book of Romans, the kingdom of God is in the holy ghost. The question is how is this possible?

First of all, we must take note that the phrase 'holy ghost' doesn't appear in the Old Testament therefore it is a New Testament concept. To understand the concept of the holy ghost we need to figure out who invented the term.

The term holy ghost first appears in the book of Matthew but Matthew isn't the first to make use of the term holy ghost because Matthew wrote his gospel after Jesus was dead and the term holy ghost appears in the gospels in red colour in some verses which means Jesus himself used the term before any apostle used it. This means that Jesus invented the term holy ghost therefore any understanding of the holy ghost that we teach must be subject to whatever Jesus meant by the 'holy ghost'.

Mark 3:29 – KJV

29. But he that shall blaspheme against the **Holy Ghost** *hath never forgiveness, but is in danger of eternal damnation:*

Mark 12:36 - KJV

*36. For David himself said by the **Holy Ghost,** The LORD said to my Lord, Sit thou on my right hand, till I make thine enemies thy footstool.*

Mark 13:11 - KJV

*11. But when they shall lead you, and deliver you up, take no thought beforehand what ye shall speak, neither do ye premeditate: but whatsoever shall be given you in that hour, that speak ye: for it is not ye that speak, but the **Holy Ghost.***

The term holy ghost is used by Jesus three times in the book of Mark. I have chosen the book of mark because it could be the earliest of the four gospels in the bible and it is widely believed amongst theologians that Mathew and Luke had taken largely from the work of Mark when they both were writing their gospels therefore the three times Jesus uses the term holy ghost in Mark can be regarded as the earliest use of the term.

Many Pentecostal and orthodox Christian movements have different views on the topic of the holy ghost and this has led to many people avoiding the topic altogether. But since Jesus appears to be the first person to use the term, then an explanation of the holy ghost that doesn't seem to share the same application of the term as Jesus used it should be discarded.

Now to answer our question on how it is possible that the kingdom of God is within you and also in the holy ghost, we need to analyse the earliest use of the term holy ghost to see if they can provide us with some clarity.

In Mark 3:29, Jesus spoke about the consequences of blaspheme against the holy ghost. However, to truly understand this passage we need to put it in the context of its whole story.

Mark 3:28-30 - KJV

28. Verily I say unto you, All sins shall be forgiven unto the sons of men, and blasphemies wherewith soever they shall blaspheme:

29. But he that shall blaspheme against the Holy Ghost hath never forgiveness, but is in danger of eternal damnation: 30. **Because they said, He hath an unclean spirit.**

You would realise that Jesus was simply responding to those who were saying that he had an unclean spirit inside him. Therefore, for Jesus to respond the way he did, he was indirectly saying that they have blasphemed against the spirit inside him which he referred to as the holy ghost.

This passage seems to accommodate both statements that the kingdom of God is within a person and that the kingdom of God is in the holy ghost. This makes sense in the sense that the holy ghost in this case was inside Jesus also. In the case of Jesus, the kingdom would be inside the holy ghost which was in turn inside Jesus.

This carries a lot of weight because this is the first time Jesus speaks about the holy ghost. He referred to the spirit inside him as the holy ghost.

The second time Jesus mentions the holy ghost is in Mark 12:36. In this verse, he was talking about king David and he said that David had functioned by the holy ghost when David made a statement in the Old Testament.

Mark 12:36 - KJV

*36. For David himself said **by the Holy Ghost,** The LORD said to my Lord, Sit thou on my right hand, till I make thine enemies thy footstool.*

This verse also seems to share a similar understanding with our previous bible verse that the holy ghost is something that resides inside a person. But this verse also seems to contradict many conventional teachings about the holy ghost. Many modern preachers claim that the holy ghost wasn't available to humans until after the death of Jesus. This begs the question; how did David get his own?

Many say that it is because David was anointed as a king that is why he had the holy ghost. But then you would also be implying that all other kings of Israel and Judah had the holy ghost also. But when you study some of the kings of the children of Israel and their evil actions, you begin to wonder why the anointing of a king did not manifest in them especially when some people argue that it was the anointing for kingship that David got from Samuel that gave him the holy ghost.

But I do not blame these pastors who teach these things in modern times. Many of the misunderstandings that exist in this generation started in the early days of modern Christianity. The church leaders then were so desperate to create one universal church that they started to edit parts of the scripture to accommodate some of their doctrines. The early Christian organisation has been accused by historians and theologians of tampering with the content of certain books of the bible so that these authors would appear to be in support of their doctrines.

One notable book that some historians think was tampered with is the gospel according to John. Although not the whole book is said to have been tampered with, the final chapters are believed to have not been written by John but they are said to have been included by the early Christian organisation to give uniformity to their beliefs. There are two bible passages that appear in the gospel of John that seem to have led to some wrong beliefs about the holy ghost.

The first of these verses is in John 7:39 but I would like to read this verse in the context of the other verses around it.

John 7:37-39 - KJV

37.   In the last day, that great day of the feast, Jesus stood and cried, saying, If any man thirst, let him come unto me, and drink.

38.   He that believeth on me, as the scripture hath said, out of his belly shall flow rivers of living water.

39.   (But this spake he of the Spirit, which they that believe on him should receive: for the Holy Ghost was not yet given; because that Jesus was not yet glorified.)

The first red flag here is that the entire verse appears in a bracket. If the original text by John was written in Hebrew, did it include a bracket or did someone add this verse to interpret the other two verses for us? Although many other verses of the bible are put in brackets, this also begs the question, was the bracket put there by the author or those who put the first bible together? If you try to understand the statements of Jesus in the upper verses, you would begin to notice a possible foul play.

In verse 37 Jesus invites people to come and drink from him, a similar statement he made to the Samaritan woman who went to fetch water. And in the case of the Samaritan woman, we discovered that he wasn't talking about ordinary water, he was talking about the word of God (truth).

In verse 38 Jesus says that he that believeth on him (Jesus) out of the belly of such persons shall flow rivers of living water. Again, we see a similar conversation in the interaction that Jesus had with the Samaritan woman where the living water is used to indicate the word of God. And if you go through the book of John, you would notice the general theme of Jesus using water and spirit to describe the word of God (the truth) therefore Jesus was just saying that anyone that believes in him would not thirst (lack understanding) again because out of his belly flows rivers of living waters (the word of God) that gives understanding. But this isn't the interpretation that was put in a bracket in verse 39. Whoever inserted verse 39 claimed he was talking about the holy spirit which also was somehow not available yet. How can Jesus be promising people something that was not yet available? Being that Jesus died several chapters later in the book of John how long were these people supposed to wait for the holy spirit if indeed Jesus was talking about the holy spirit? So, in my opinion, chapter 39 was wrongfully inserted into the book of John.

John 4:13-14 - KJV

13. Jesus answered and said unto her, Whosoever drinketh of this water shall thirst again:

14. But whosoever drinketh of the water that I shall give him shall never thirst; but the water that I shall give him shall be in him a well of water springing up into everlasting life.

But to say that he was talking about the holy ghost that was not yet given, then you would be saying that Jesus was still owing the Samaritan woman her living water that she would have to wait for him to die first before she gets it.

To say that the holy ghost was not yet given is to contradict Peter also. Because like Jesus, Peter also stated people who functioned by the holy ghost in the Old Testament.

2 Peter 1:21 - KJV

*21.   For the prophecy came not in old time by the will of man: but holy men of God spake as they were moved by the **Holy Ghost.***

If the holy ghost was only made available by the death of Jesus, then how did the prophets of old get it? When you consider how many prophets existed in the Old Testament you begin to wonder how many people had the holy ghost already. In fact, at some point, Jezebel killed so many prophets that a certain man called Obadiah was still able to hide 100 prophets in a cave. If these prophets were operating by the holy ghost, then just how many people had access to the holy ghost?

1 Kings 18:4 - KJV

4. For it was so, when Jezebel cut off the prophets of the LORD, that Obadiah took an hundred prophets, and hid them by fifty in a cave, and fed them with bread and water.)

Or was it only selected prophets that were functioning by the holy ghost? There is no way to prove that only a few prophets had the holy ghost.

The other verse in the book of John that has raised eyebrows about the concept of the holy ghost is in John 20:21

John 20:22 - KJV

22. And when he had said this, he breathed on them, and saith unto them, Receive ye the Holy Ghost:

This is one of the verses in the concluding chapters of the book of John that make historians suspect foul play. The idea is that the holy spirit is imparted by one person to another. I see this as an attempt by early Christian leaders to force their doctrines by disguising them as the works of John. This is suspicious because, in most of John's letters in the bible, he hardly teaches about the holy spirit. Except for the two verses we are addressing, he only writes about the holy spirit three times. Even Peter another apostle of Jesus only talks about it once.

There are other parts of this chapter 20 of John that makes people question its authenticity. First, let's look at the next verse after verse 22.

John 20:23 - KJV

23.   Whose soever sins ye remit, they are remitted unto them; and whose soever sins ye retain, they are retained.

This is an attempt to say that Jesus gave the leaders of the church the power to absorb people of their sins. This is an attempt to justify a certain doctrine of the early Christian organisation that put the bible together. This was done to justify the claim by the early modern Christian organisation that the fathers and priests of the church can absorb people of their sins. This is incoherent with the teaching of how to become born again by Jesus. Where he states that it is the truth that would make a person free from sin (not the priest or his disciples).

Another suspicious verse in this chapter is verse 14 where it is stated that Mary Magdalene saw Jesus at his tomb but could not recognise him. This to any rational mind does not make sense because she practically lived and worked with Jesus for a huge part of his ministry.

So how come she couldn't recognise him. Many historians still doubt if John ever wrote about the aftermath of the death of Jesus. But because this would raise a lot of questions concerning why no disciple of Jesus wrote about the aftermath of his death, it seems that those who put the bible together chose to write one for John. I said no disciple wrote so because the writers of the other three gospels were not disciples only one (Mark) was a Jew who is said to have been a close friend of Peter. The other two authors Mathew and Luke were not Jews and never met Jesus in person or worked with any of his direct disciples.

This is not to cast doubt on the entire bible but to make you understand that when trying to understand the gospel, you must make sure that whatever you take in must be in unison with the teachings of Jesus. The teachings credited to apostles must be in line with one another and in line with the teachings of Jesus. If you see anything that is not in line, it needs broader studying before you can verify it. After all, Jesus is the foundation of the gospel that any Christian should teach.

Hebrew 12:2 - KJV

2.   Looking unto Jesus the author and finisher of our faith; who for the joy that was set before him endured the cross, despising the shame, and is set down at the right hand of the throne of God.

What we can therefore conclude here is that the holy ghost that Jesus was talking about had been in operation and available to man since the Old Testament. Also, the holy ghost resides in a person as our third verse of interest in the book of Mark seems to indicate. It also indicates that the holy ghost can function through an individual. Like it did with Jesus and the prophets in the Old Testament. Like in this next verse, Jesus was telling his disciples to allow the holy ghost to speak through them. This also begs the question, if the holy ghost was not available till the death of Jesus, how was the holy ghost meant to speak through the disciples of Jesus?

Mark 13:11 - KJV

11. But when they shall lead you, and deliver you up, take no thought beforehand what ye shall speak, neither do ye premeditate: but whatsoever shall be given you in that hour, that speak ye: for it is not ye that speak, but the Holy Ghost.

But really how is the kingdom of God in the holy ghost as well as a person especially if you examine that when Jesus said the kingdom of God is within you, he was talking to Pharisees not even his disciples or modern born-again Christians who think they are the only ones who have access to the holy ghost.

Luke 17:20-21 - KJV

20.   And when he was demanded of the Pharisees, when the kingdom of God should come, he answered them and said, The kingdom of God cometh not with observation:

21.   Neither shall they say, Lo here! or, lo there! for, behold, the kingdom of God is within you.

Also, when Jesus was teaching about the kingdom of God being at hand, he was teaching a general crowd not only his disciples. This means that if everyone has access to the kingdom of God, then everyone has access to the holy ghost. Because the kingdom of God is also in the holy ghost as stated in Romans 14:17.

Mark 1:14-15 - KJV

14.   Now after that John was put in prison, Jesus came into Galilee, preaching the gospel of the kingdom of God,

15.   And saying, The time is fulfilled, and the kingdom of God is at hand: repent ye, and believe the gospel.

This means that the holy ghost is inside everyone like it must have been inside the people at Galilee that is why Jesus told them that the kingdom of God is at hand (in their possession) and it must have been inside the Pharisees when Jesus said the kingdom of God is within them. But it seems that the holy ghost manifests in people at different levels if it even manifests at all in some people.

Since righteousness, peace, and joy are in the holy ghost, and the holy ghost manifests in different people at different levels at different times, then righteousness, peace, and joy will also be expressed in different people at different levels at different times. Thus, the more the holy ghost is expressed, the more righteousness, peace, and joy will be expressed.

But how come the holy ghost is inside everyone from the apostles to the Pharisees to the people at Galilee to the prophets of old, and Jesus himself?

To answer this question, we would need to understand Man as a concept.

MAN

To effectively analyse the man, we would have to go back to the very beginning of his existence or the very first mention of him, the moment God had the idea of man in the book of Genesis as written by Moses.

Genesis 1:26 - KJV

26. And God said, Let us make man in our image, after our likeness: and let them have dominion over the fish of the sea, and over the fowl of the air, and over the cattle, and over all the earth, and over every creeping thing that creepeth upon the earth.

Although many Christians have made up their minds concerning the big question mark concerning verse 26 of chapter one of Genesis. The big question which has largely remained unanswered in my opinion is, who was God talking to when he said "let us make man in our image"?

Many Christians believe that God was talking to the other two persons in the trinity. They argue that God the father was talking to God the Son and God the holy spirit. But I disagree with this belief because the idea of God as a trinity was introduced later in the New Testament. Therefore, Moses's writing could not have been built on a concept that only came into existence a long time after he had already been dead. If he was aware of God as a trinity then he definitely would have somehow referred to this somewhere else in his writings. But since there is no mention of God as a trinity by Moses, then we will just be religious to assume that Moses was referring to the trinity when God said "let us make man in our image" in Genesis 1:26.

If it seems irresponsible to assume it was the trinity communicating within themselves in the beginning then we must seek to unravel the identity of the other beings God was talking to when he said "let us make man in our image" in Genesis 1:26.

The answer to this question has been staring at us for many years since whenever the first bible was printed. But how we missed something so obvious is a mystery on its own. The answer is in the previous verses that precede Genesis 1:26. The answer to the identity of who God was talking to when he said Let us make man in our image can be found between Genesis 1:20 to Genesis 1:25. Let's take time to digest these verses.

Genesis 1:20-25 - KJV

20.   And God said, Let the **waters** bring forth abundantly the moving creature that hath life, and fowl that may fly above the earth in the open firmament of heaven.

21.   And God created great whales, and every living creature that moveth, which the waters brought forth abundantly, after their kind, and every winged fowl after his kind: and God saw that it was good.

22.   And God blessed them, saying, Be fruitful, and multiply, and fill the waters in the seas, and let fowl multiply in the earth.

23.   And the evening and the morning were the fifth day.

24.   And God said, Let the **earth** bring forth the living creature after his kind, cattle, and creeping thing, and beast of the earth after his kind: and it was so.

25.   And God made the beast of the earth after his kind, and cattle after their kind, and every thing that creepeth upon the earth after his kind: and God saw that it was good.

Many people did not notice one obvious fact which is before Genesis 1:26, God was already speaking to two entities which are the Waters (in verse 20) and the Earth (in verse 24). God was talking to the Waters and the Earth from verse 20 to verse 25, discussing the creation of other creatures and then God proceeds to say "let us make man in our image". The only explanation that makes sense is that God was talking to the Waters and the Earth. This adds up when you consider the fact that the human body was made from the Water and the Earth in Genesis 2:6-7.

Genesis 2:6-7 - KJV

*6.   But there went up a **mist** from the earth, and **watered** the whole face of the **ground.***

7.   And the LORD God formed man of the dust of the ground, and breathed into his nostrils the breath of life; and man became a living soul.

Notice that in verse 6 the mist (water) watered the whole face of the ground (Earth) for God to form man. The Waters and the Earth did not need to be reminded or instructed to provide their elements for the forming of the flesh, they already knew their role to play because they had been informed in Genesis 1:26. The question then becomes, what was God's contribution to the making of man especially if he said "let us make man in our image" to the Waters and the Earth. What did God bring to the table? The answer is in the next verse after Genesis 1:26.

Genesis 1:27 - KJV

*27. So God **created** man in his own image, in the image of God created he him; male and female created he them.*

In this verse 27, God proceeds to create man in his image but this should raise eyebrows because, in the previous verse, he just agreed with the Water and the Earth that they should make man in their combined image and likeness. So was God being fraudulent, did he break an agreement that he came up with by himself? After agreeing with the Water and the Earth why would God go on and do something by himself? The answer is in the word "**create**"

In verse 26 God said "Let us **make** man in our image" but in verse 27 God **created** man in his image. This must mean that there is a difference between making something and creating something. Therefore, let us consider the definitions of both words and see what the difference might be.

MAKE:

To form (something) by putting parts together or combining substances

CREATE:

To bring (something) into existence.

Although people most times interchange the two words, here is the difference.

To make something, you have to make use of pre-existing materials, but to create something is to bring it out of nothing. This means you don't need any pre-existing ingredients for creation to take place. This makes sense if you factor in the modern use of the word create. A person is referred to as being creative if they are used to bringing up ideas or opportunities from scratch (out of nothing). An example of this is a storyteller who cooks up fictional scenarios out of nothing or in sports terms, a person is considered creative if they can produce opportunities or plays out of nothing.

On the other hand, to make anything requires the use of already existing elements. A good example is the making of a car. To make a car requires the use of already existing metals and steel for body parts, the use of already existing leather for the interior of the car and already existing rubber for the tyres and many other already existing materials to make various parts that are brought together and used to form the car.

In most cases creation and making usually go together only that creation always comes before the making of a thing.

A good example would be a movie, the story is first created before it is made. The making part of the movie involves putting the created story into real-life acts and props. Therefore, the movie undergoes creation before it is made.

Another example can be a car, the idea of the car is first created by drafting out its design and specs and all the components before it undergoes the process of being made. The making involves bringing together pre-existing materials to form the car.

One can argue that the movie or the car already existed although not physically before they were put into physical forms. Practically everything is first created before being made. Practically everything can be said to exist spiritually before they exist physically, this is why many philosophers argue that it's the spiritual that gives birth to the physical. even every action firstly exists spiritually as thoughts before they are acted out physically or put into form.

This same principle is demonstrated in the case of the first man in Genesis 1:27 man existed as a spirit being not physically because man was only formed physically in Genesis 2:6-7

Genesis 2:6-7 - KJV

6.   But there went up a mist from the earth, and watered the whole face of the ground.

*7.   And the LORD God **formed** man of the dust of the ground, and breathed into his nostrils the breath of life; and man became a living soul.*

The proof that man existed as a spiritual being will be found in Genesis 1:27-31 because immediately God created man, God started communicating with him. If man did not already exist in one form or the other, God would not be able to communicate with him.

Genesis 1:27-31 - KJV

27.   So God created man in his own image, in the image of God created he him; male and female created he them.

*28.   And God blessed them, and God **said** unto them, Be fruitful, and multiply, and replenish the earth, and subdue it: and have dominion over the fish of the sea, and over the fowl of the air, and over every living thing that moveth upon the earth.*

*29.   And God **said,** Behold, I have given you every herb bearing seed, which is upon the face of all the earth, and every tree, in the which is the fruit of a tree yielding seed; to you it shall be for meat.*

30.   And to every beast of the earth, and to every fowl of the air, and to every thing that creepeth upon the earth, wherein there is life, I have given every green herb for meat: and it was so.

31.   And God saw every thing that he had made, and, behold, it was very good. And the evening and the morning were the sixth day.

God was even instructing man before he existed physically. This is proof enough that man existed as a spiritual being. Another argument that will show that man existed as a spiritual being is that man was created in the image of God in Genesis 1:27 therefore what is the image of God? The answer can be found in John 4:24.

John 4:24 - KJV

*24.   God is a **Spirit:** and they that worship him must worship him in spirit and in truth.*

God is a spirit, this is why no one has seen God physically therefore if man was created in the image of God, then man had to have been a spirit before he had a body in Genesis 2:7.

The point I am driving at is that man is originally a spirit. The question is how and why did he get his body(flesh)? This is a question that we have answered already through Genesis 2:6-7 where God formed(made) the man physically using the Water and the Earth.

Genesis 2:6-7 - KJV

*6.   But there went up a **mist** from the earth, and **watered** the whole face of the **ground.***

7.   And the LORD God formed man of the dust of the ground, and breathed into his nostrils the breath of life; and man became a living soul.

It is at this point that the flesh of man was formed, and the making of man was completed when God breathed into the flesh. The most logical explanation for this is that God breathing into the body of the man was him putting the man (spirit) into the flesh.

One other thing to note about man as a spirit is that there are two types of spirit as man and these are the male spirit and the female spirit. They are both created in the image of God (spirit).

Genesis 1:27 - KJV

So God created man in his own image, in the image of God created he him; male and female created he them.

If man is created as a spirit in the image of God, then that spirit will have the ability to function like God. That spirit must have been holy. That spirit must have come with the kingdom/life/character of God. That spirit therefore qualifies to be the holy ghost.

This justifies Jesus claiming that we all have the kingdom of God inside of us. This automatically means that we all carry the holy ghost inside of us, and this means that we all have the capacity for righteousness, peace, and joy inside of us.

But like we said, it is to the extent to which the holy spirit is manifesting that we will experience righteousness, peace, and joy.

Therefore, since we are experiencing a scarcity of righteousness, peace, and joy, then we can say that the holy ghost is rarely manifesting in people these days. But why is this the case especially if every human is carrying the holy ghost inside of them?

The answer is the flesh.

After man was created, he was given the flesh. As time has gone on, man (the spirit) has grown increasingly silent while the flesh has taken control of most of the desires and activities. The flesh has now overshadowed the spirit man.

Therefore, we will need to take a look at the flesh to understand why and how the flesh is causing the spirit to be silent and powerless.

THE FLESH

If man is a spirit put into a body referred to as his flesh, then we must understand his flesh also. Many religious people blame man's flesh for his inability to stay righteous but it's hard to counter such arguments especially when man never fell or sinned against God until he was in a flesh. However, the danger with the above view is that one will tend to see the flesh as a curse only but this wouldn't be right especially when it was God that thought up the idea of the flesh and formed it in Genesis 2:7 this means there must have been a reason for the flesh. God must have had a good reason for the flesh coming into existence. Thus, we would be wrong to view the flesh as a curse.

To this end, we must seek to understand the flesh and its relationship with man, how the two were designed to function together by God. Firstly, we must start with why God made/formed the flesh.

We already know from our previous chapter that God first thought about the flesh in Genesis 1:26 when he first told the Waters and the Earth "let us make man in our image"

Genesis 1:26 - KJV

26.   And God said, Let us make man in our image, after our likeness: and let them have dominion over the fish of the sea, and over the fowl of the air, and over the cattle, and over all the earth, and over every creeping thing that creepeth upon the earth.

The reason why God wanted to make man is also contained in the above. God's reason was "let them have dominion over the fish of the sea, and over the fouls of the air, and over the cattle, and over all the earth, and over every creeping thing that creepeth upon the earth".

God had already made plans with the Waters and the Earth in Genesis 1:20-25 on making many other creatures that were to exist on the planet. God needed to create a being that can oversee all of his creations including the Earth and its vegetation. This being is man.

Genesis 1:20-25 - KJV

20.   And God said, Let the waters bring forth abundantly the moving creature that hath life, and fowl that may fly above the earth in the open firmament of heaven.

21.   And God created great whales, and every living creature that moveth, which the waters brought forth abundantly, after their kind, and every winged fowl after his kind: and God saw that it was good.

22.   And God blessed them, saying, Be fruitful, and multiply, and fill the waters in the seas, and let fowl multiply in the earth.

23.   And the evening and the morning were the fifth day.

24.   And God said, Let the earth bring forth the living creature after his kind, cattle, and creeping thing, and beast of the earth after his kind: and it was so.

25.   And God made the beast of the earth after his kind, and cattle after their kind, and every thing that creepeth upon the earth after his kind: and God saw that it was good.

Immediately after concluding plans with the Waters and the Earth for other creatures in verse 25, he starts his plans for man. The question becomes why did God also need the participation of the Earth and the Waters in the making of man? After all, God had allowed the Waters and the Earth to have autonomy on the design and creation of other creatures by telling them to "bring fort creatures after their kind" so why did he need to discuss man with the Waters and the Earth?

Remember we concluded in the last chapter that God is a spirit thus creating man after his image means that man will be a spirit. But the

Waters and the Earth are physical entities thus anything fashioned from them has to end up physical. If man who is a spirit must be able to oversee the other creatures, then he must do so in a form that would enable him to manage these physical creatures thus he would need a body with which he can relate to the creatures from the Waters and the Earth and the vegetation of the Earth also. To this end the Waters and the Earth would need to provide their elements for man's physical existence; elements used to make the flesh. Thus, the flesh was formed for purely good reasons. The proof of this is in the early verses of Genesis chapter two.

Genesis 2:1-5 - KJV

1.   Thus the heavens and the earth were finished, and all the host of them.

2.   And on the seventh day God ended his work which he had made; and he rested on the seventh day from all his work which he had made.

3.   And God blessed the seventh day, and sanctified it: because that in it he had rested from all his work which God created and made.

4.   These are the generations of the heavens and of the earth when they were created, in the day that the LORD God made the earth and the heavens,

5.   And every plant of the field before it was in the earth, and every herb of the field before it grew: for the LORD God had not caused it to rain upon the earth, and there was not a man to till the ground.

If you pay close attention to the verses above, you would realise that God's plan for managing the affairs on the earth and manifesting his will on earth was man. That is why he did not allow rain to fall until there was a man to physically tend to the earth. Man would need the flesh to exist in the physical and execute God's will and intentions for his creations. Both the Waters and the Earth understood their role in the making of Man and the need for the flesh for man. This is why in verse six of Genesis chapter two, the Waters and the Earth did not need to be told or need to be reminded of their roles, they went into action to provide elements for God to form a flesh for man. They were already onboard with God's plan to make man in Genesis 1:26.

Genesis 2:6-7 - KJV

6.   But there went up a mist from the earth, and watered the whole face of the ground.

7.   And the LORD God formed man of the dust of the ground, and breathed into his nostrils the breath of life; and man became a living soul.

If God's intention for giving man the flesh was genuinely good, then can the flesh be exonerated from any blame in the fall of man and man's sin? The answer is no.

There are two fundamental challenges that man would have to face because of the flesh he now inhabits. One has to do with the nature of the flesh, the other has to do with the source of the flesh.

The nature of the flesh is one that is riddled with imperfection anything that is gotten from the physical can't be perfect, it would be subject to errors and also wear and tear. Things that exist spiritually can be perfect until one tries to put them in physical form. Let us make use of the examples of a car and a movie, both first exist spiritually in the forms of a design and a story respectively and as long as they stay that way, they can be considered perfect. The imperfection starts to show when physical elements are brought into the equation to give form to the car and the movie.

In the case of the car, the imperfections are in the nature of the physical elements used in making the car. The leather would someday succumb to heat, the tyre would deplete and could burst one day, the engine will break down due to wear and tear someday, the body parts would rust someday, the glasses can break, etc. no matter how perfect the design is, once it takes on a physical form, it is exposed to imperfections.

The same can be said for a movie, the story could be superbly airtight and interesting, it can have a good balance of suspense and emotion and all the right things it needs to make it a good story, but once you try to put it in physical form by making the story, you inherit imperfection. The imperfection can be in form of bad acting, lack of the right voice tones, props not being perfect, etc. in fact when it comes to the physical realm nothing can be perfect because you are introducing elements made from the Waters and the Earth, two entities that can't be perfect. The only things that can be perfect are spiritual in nature.

Everything physical is subject to subjective evaluation also thus perfection is not possible. The colour of a car might be right for one person and wrong for the other. The colour of a car might be right for a person today and not right for the same person tomorrow. Thus, the idea of perfection is impossible for anything physical. Thus, the nature of things physical is flawed by imperfection and the only way out of this is contentment. To be contented with the best that you can get out of anything physical per time because it can never be perfect.

The question becomes how does this affect man? We know now that man is a spirit in the image of God who also is a spirit. But in other for man to function in the physical, he had to put on a body from this physical realm thus he was given a flesh fashioned out of the two physical sources Water and Earth. This means that the nature of the flesh the man is given would be that of the nature of the Waters and the Earth. Thus, the nature of the flesh can never be perfect. A person can't have everything perfect in his body. You can't have perfect eyes, perfect teeth, perfect fingernails, or any other body part, for the same reasons a car or a movie can't be perfect. One of the reasons the flesh can't be perfect is wear and tear. All physical elements are subject to wear and tear that forces some unwanted transformation over time no matter how well you try to preserve it. This is why the human body must age and undergo unwanted transformation just like the body of a car, a fish, a door, etc. The best one can do for any physical property he/she owns is to manage it properly so it doesn't become a liability faster than it should. The same applies to the human body.

The other thing that makes the human body imperfect, is that just like the body of a car it is subject to subjective valuation. The colour of a body can be right to a person but its height won't be right. It can be right today and wrong tomorrow. This is why it is said that humans can't be satisfied. The colour of a person's fingernail today might not be nice again tomorrow thus the flesh can't be perceived as perfect.

This brings us to the second issue with the flesh asides imperfection which is its source. We have understood that everything physical is sourced from either the Waters or the Earth or a combination of both most times which is the case of the human body. While the Man himself is created in the image of God, the body is in the image of the Waters and the Earth. This means the Man and his body will have different programming. While the man (the spirit) is prone to think more like God and inherit the same desires and urges that God has, the flesh on the other hand will inherit its desires and taste from the Waters and the Earth. This is because the source of the Man (the spirit) is God but the source of the flesh is a combination of the Waters and the Earth. The Man will be more able to relate to spiritual things because he is a spiritual being but the flesh will be more able to relate to physical things. This will cause a conflict of interest because their value systems are not heading in the same direction. While the Man will build his value system on spiritual pleasures like joy, peace and fulfilment, the flesh will build its value system on physical gratifications and attractions (earthly material things). While the Man will long after spiritual gifts from God, the flesh will long after material things from this realm like cars, houses, wrist watches because these are the things it can relate with. After all, these material things are made out of the same elements that the flesh was made from (the Water and the Earth). The spirit (man) can't drive a car thus can't directly get pleasure from the car, it is the flesh that drives the car, and wear wristwatches and flashy material things, thus these are the things that the flesh would be naturally drawn to.

This conflict of interest and value system that exists between the man and the flesh due to their different sources, is one that the man would have to deal with as long as he is stuck with a body.

The result of this conflict between the man and his flesh is that one would have to bow to the other. Either the flesh succumbs to the will of the spirit (the man) which ultimately is the will of God, or the man (the spirit) succumbs to the will of the flesh which is subject to material gratifications from material things.

While the spirit will be more interested in the companionship and partnership it can get out of the opposite gender, the flesh will base its attraction to the opposite gender on physical gratification like physical features and sexual activities. The same desire for the opposite gender but the value sort by the man and his flesh are different. Thus, the man will have to contend to make sure his value system overshadows the value system of his flesh.

Without being tied to the flesh, the man (spirit) would never go against the will of God because he is created in the image and likeness of God. But once the spirit has been put inside a flesh, it can now be tempted to stray away from the will and desire of God by the desires of the flesh. The evidence to this is in the fact that God never warned man about any action that could derail him from God's will until man had been given a body. God knew that the presence of the flesh now poses a threat to man's ability to stick to the will and desires of God. Thus, man was never capable of sin until he got a body in Genesis 2:7 thus God had to give him a warning on what to avoid now that he was housed in a flesh.

Genesis 2:16-17 - KJV

16.   And the LORD God commanded the man, saying, Of every tree of the garden thou mayest freely eat:

17.   But of the tree of the knowledge of good and evil, thou shalt not eat of it: for in the day that thou eatest thereof thou shalt surely die.

Man did not need any warning until this time because he had no flesh to distract him.

One other thing to know is that there is a difference between the words Man and Human. Man is a spirit in the image of God. You must know that spirits have no colour (hue). The word human is consisting of two words one is hue, and the other is man. Thus, the word human can be translated as coloured-man which refers to the flesh. So, when social scientists say humans are insatiable, they are referring to the flesh which means they are correct if you factor in what we have discussed in this chapter.

The problem here is that the flesh is constantly at war with the spirit in the sense that it is always trying to be in control and overshadow the spirit. This constant battle is one that is highlighted in the book of Romans.

Romans 7:21-24 - KJV

21.   I find then a law, that, when I would do good, evil is present with me.

22.   For I delight in the law of God after the inward man:

23.   But I see another law in my members, warring against the law of my mind, and bringing me into captivity to the law of sin which is in my members.

24.   O wretched man that I am! who shall deliver me from the body of this death?

The author of Romans tries to highlight the presence of two different value systems within a human being. One value system belongs to the inward man (spirit man) and another value system belongs to the members of his body (his flesh). This conflict of interest is one that Man (the spirit) has to deal with as a result of being attached to the flesh. This conflict of interest or value system now makes it possible for man (as a soul) to sin (derail from the will and value system of God).

The more the flesh wins this battle, the more a person is led by his/her flesh into fulfilling the desires of the flesh and less of the desires of the spirit. In this case, the spirit (the holy ghost) is seldom manifesting its righteousness, peace, and joy. But if the spirit is more in control, the more of manifestation of righteousness, peace, and joy we would see and less of the desires of the flesh we would see.

Galatians 5:16 - KJV

16.   This I say then, Walk in the Spirit, and ye shall not fulfil the lust of the flesh.

The question becomes, how does one walk in the spirit?

The answer is simple, chase after righteousness, peace, and joy (the kingdom of God).

Matthew 6:33 - KJV

*33.   But seek ye first the **kingdom of God,** and his righteousness; and all these things shall be added unto you.*

This should empower the spirit to have more control over our lives than the flesh does. But this is a constant battle as the book of Romans has pointed out and also Jesus pointed out that getting the kingdom of God (righteousness, peace, and joy) would not be a simple task, there has to be some effort put into it.

Romans 7:21-24 - KJV

21.   I find then a law, that, when I would do good, evil is present with me.

22.   For I delight in the law of God after the inward man:

23.   But I see another law in my members, warring against the law of my mind, and bringing me into captivity to the law of sin which is in my members.

24.   O wretched man that I am! who shall deliver me from the body of this death?

Matthew 11:12 - KJV

12.   And from the days of John the Baptist until now the kingdom of heaven suffereth violence, and the violent take it by force.

If the kingdom of God is in the holy ghost, then these verses are just saying that it is not an easy task to allow the holy ghost to manifest.

But I can show you a sure way to express the kingdom of God and allow the holy ghost to manifest in your life. This is why I have written this book. To show you how you can easily activate the manifestations of the spirit starting from righteousness.

RIGHTEOUSNESS

David in the bible was one man who seemed to know the secret to righteousness.

Psalms 111:10 - KJV

*10.   The fear of the LORD is the beginning of wisdom: a good **understanding** have all they that do his commandments: his praise endureth for ever.*

Psalms 119:34 - KJV

*34.   Give me **understanding,** and I shall keep thy law; yea, I shall observe it with my whole heart.*

David seems to believe that the secret ingredient to keeping the commandments of God and being righteous.

When it comes to keeping the commandments of God, many people struggle to do so simply because they have not understood the commandments and why they exist., many people have not understood that the commandments of God are for their own good, not God's.

A good example is someone who lies and does not realize that it is his own reputation and credibility at stake, not God's.

Another example is fornication. People who disobey this do not fully grasp the consequences of their actions both to their soul and their body. God will never be at risk of any sexually transmitted disease. It is the fornicator at risk. God is never at risk of a broken marriage or relationship or broken heart. It is always the perpetrator of fornication or adultery.

There are other things to understand that will help one stay righteous easily, but the basic understanding of this is that being righteous is not for God's benefit but Man's.

Many people think that the commandments are in place for God's benefit because of the way they have been taught. They do not understand that the only reason your unrighteousness displeases God, is because he loves you and can't stand watching the consequences you have to face because of your unrighteousness.

Part of being righteous (accessing/living by grace) is being able to overcome temptations. So, if we say having understanding is the way to righteousness/grace, then understanding must also be a way to overcome temptations.

Let us examine the very first temptation in the bible (the temptation of Eve) and see if an understanding could have helped.

Genesis 3:1-7 - KJV

1.   Now the serpent was more subtle than any beast of the field which the LORD God had made. And he said unto the woman, Yea, hath God said, Ye shall not eat of every tree of the garden?
2.   And the woman said unto the serpent, We may eat of the fruit of the trees of the garden:
3.   But of the fruit of the tree which is in the midst of the garden, God hath said, Ye shall not eat of it, neither shall ye touch it, lest ye die.
4.   And the serpent said unto the woman, Ye shall not surely die:
5.   For God doth know that in the day ye eat thereof, then your eyes shall be opened, and ye shall be as gods, knowing good and evil.
6.   And when the woman saw that the tree was good for food, and that it was pleasant to the eyes, and a tree to be desired to make one wise, she took of the fruit thereof, and did eat, and gave also unto her husband with her; and he did eat.
7.   And the eyes of them both were opened, and they knew that they were naked; and they sewed fig leaves together, and made themselves aprons.

In this temptation, all the serpent did was trick the woman that if she eats from the tree of knowledge of good and evil, she will be like gods (verse 5). But this was a trick because there was no need for Eve to want to be like gods. After all, in chapter one of Genesis, it is said that she was already created in the image of the almighty God. But the serpent was able to paint becoming a god (take note of the small letter g) as a step forward for Eve.

Genesis 1:27 - KJV

*27. So God **created** man in his own image, in the image of God created he him; male and female created he them.*

The only reason why Eve fell for this is that she was ignorant to the fact that she was already in the image of the almighty God. At the time God decided to create man in His image, man was not in existence thus the only beings that knew that man was created in the image of God are whoever God was speaking to in Genesis 1:26.

Genesis 1:26 - KJV

26. And God said, Let us make man in our image, after our likeness: and let them have dominion over the fish of the sea, and over the fowl of the air, and over the cattle, and over all the earth, and over every creeping thing that creepeth upon the earth.

Let's assume that Eve had already been told that she was created in the image of God, she could still have fallen for the temptation because there is a difference between knowing and understanding. So perhaps Eve did not understand how she was created in the image of God.

Many of us still lack this understanding until this day. Whenever we hear that we are created in the image of God, we automatically think that God looks physically the way we do. But that would be wrong considering that there are many imperfections in our physical body. God can't be said to have such imperfections.

So how then are we created in the image of God?

To understand this, we have to know what the image of God is.

John 4:24 - KJV

*24.   God is a **Spirit:** and they that worship him must worship him in spirit and in truth.*

God is a spirit, this is why no one has seen God physically therefore if man was created in the image of God, then man had to have been a spirit. Only that man was given a body in Genesis 2:7.

Genesis 2:6-7 - KJV

*8.   But there went up a **mist** from the earth, and **watered** the whole face of the **ground.***
9.   And the LORD God formed man of the dust of the ground, and breathed into his nostrils the breath of life; and man became a living soul.

So, the serpent was only able to get Eve because Eve did not understand how she was created in the image of God. That it was a spiritual resemblance to God not physical. If she had thought that her resemblance to God was physical then that explains why it was easy to convince her that that wasn't enough because when it comes to our physical body, there are too many flaws and limitations to be able to prove that we are in the image of God.

This is why even to this day many Christians struggle to have complete confidence that they are in the image of God because they do not understand that it's not a physical image but a spiritual one. We do not understand that Man is a spiritual being like God only that man is housed in a physical container called the flesh. Many people do not understand that we are not our flesh.

Eve's righteousness failed because she lacked understanding. This shows that there is no righteousness without understanding.

Another example of temptation is the one joseph faced in the house of Potiphar. Potiphar's wife tried to seduce Joseph into sexual immorality but Joseph ran away even leaving his garment behind.

Genesis 39:7 - 12 - KJV

7.   And it came to pass after these things, that his master's wife cast her eyes upon Joseph; and she said, Lie with me.

8.   But he refused, and said unto his master's wife, Behold, my master wotteth not what is with me in the house, and he hath committed all that he hath to my hand;

9.   There is none greater in this house than I; neither hath he kept back any thing from me but thee, because thou art his wife: how then can I do this great wickedness, and sin against God?

10.   And it came to pass, as she spake to Joseph day by day, that he hearkened not unto her, to lie by her, or to be with her.

11.   And it came to pass about this time, that Joseph went into the house to do his business; and there was none of the men of the house there within.

12.   And she caught him by his garment, saying, Lie with me: and he left his garment in her hand, and fled, and got him out.

What saved Joseph in this temptation was that he understood that when it comes to sexual urges, the surest way to overcome is to flee(run). Don't even think about trusting your flesh in such situations, run while you still have the will to.

1 Corinthians 6:18 - KJV

18.   Flee fornication. Every sin that a man doeth is without the body; but he that committeth fornication sinneth against his own body.

2 Timothy 2:22 - KJV

22.   Flee also youthful lusts: but follow righteousness, faith, charity, peace, with them that call on the Lord out of a pure heart.

Unfortunately, many people do not understand this rule. They constantly stick around sexual temptations, trusting that they can handle them until they fall and start regretting their decisions.

Jesus was another person who used understanding to overcome temptation. His understanding of the scriptures he had read, and his understanding of what is important in life was what he used to overcome his temptations.

Matthew 4:1-10 - KJV

1.   Then was Jesus led up of the Spirit into the wilderness to be tempted of the devil.
2.   And when he had fasted forty days and forty nights, he was afterward an hungred.

3.   And when the tempter came to him, he said, If thou be the Son of God, command that these stones be made bread.

4.   But he answered and said, It is written, Man shall not live by bread alone, but by every word that proceedeth out of the mouth of God.

5.   Then the devil taketh him up into the holy city, and setteth him on a pinnacle of the temple,

6.   And saith unto him, If thou be the Son of God, cast thyself down: for it is written, He shall give his angels charge concerning thee: and in their hands they shall bear thee up, lest at any time thou dash thy foot against a stone.

7.   Jesus said unto him, It is written again, Thou shalt not tempt the Lord thy God.

8.   Again, the devil taketh him up into an exceeding high mountain, and sheweth him all the kingdoms of the world, and the glory of them;

9.   And saith unto him, All these things will I give thee, if thou wilt fall down and worship me.

10.   Then saith Jesus unto him, Get thee hence, Satan: for it is written, Thou shalt worship the Lord thy God, and him only shalt thou serve.

Most temptations occur like arguments or debates either in your head or with someone else. And if you lack knowledge and understanding, it is very difficult to win these debates. This means that without understanding, it is impossible to stay righteous.

PEACE

Peace is the second characteristic of the kingdom of God as stated by the book of Romans.

Romans 14:17 - KJV

17. For the kingdom of God is not meat and drink; but righteousness, and peace, and joy in the Holy Ghost.

What many have not realized is that these three elements of the kingdom/nature of God exist co-dependently. They go hand in hand, righteousness gives birth to peace which gives birth to Joy.

This means that if understanding is a prerequisite for righteousness, it is also a prerequisite for peace.

Let us try to establish if this is the case in reality.

Peace is defined as freedom from disturbance.

The question now becomes; how is righteousness related to freedom from disturbance.

To answer this question, we would have to examine how the lack of peace and unrighteousness are related.

If you take a closer look at many of the temptations in the bible, you would realise that when the devil wants to make someone do evil, he would first do or say something to trouble the mind of that person.

Let's take a look at the temptation of Eve, the serpent said to her, that if she doesn't eat from the tree of knowledge of good and evil, she wouldn't be like the gods. Trying to put the fear that she wasn't good enough inside her at the same time taking away her peace of mind.

Genesis 3:4-5 - KJV

4. And the serpent said unto the woman, Ye shall not surely die:

5. For God doth know that in the day ye eat thereof, then your eyes shall be opened, and ye shall be as gods, knowing good and evil.

Once she allowed that statement to sink into her mind and take away her peace, she would do whatever it takes to try and gain that peace back. But this time, the most likely action was to eat from the tree of knowledge of good and evil in hopes that she can become like the gods and start to feel good about herself again.

The same thing would have happened with Joseph if he had allowed his master's wife's advancement for sex to disturb his peace. Joseph could have thought about all the negative things that could happen if he rejects Potiphar's wife. He could have thought about the possibility that she might request for him to lose his job, or that she might take away his privileges in the house or she would start picking on him, or that she would accuse him falsely of different things he didn't do (which she eventually did). If he had pondered on these things and allowed them to take away his peace of mind, then most likely he would have sinned.

But Joseph understood that the solution to this kind of situation is to flee. If he had stayed longer and allowed these thoughts to dwell in his mind, then the likelihood of him sinning would increase. His understanding saved him from unrighteousness because his understanding helped him maintain peace in his mind.

In the case of Jesus, the tempter tried to use the same tactic that was used on Eve. The tempter showed Jesus the riches of this world and tried to sell him the fear that he was missing out. That Jesus could use his gifts for his selfish gains by turning the stone to bread. This kind of conversation can be very disturbing to the mind. A person can lose his/her peace of mind after such conversations and once that happens, the likelihood of that person doing something unrighteous is high.

But like in the case of Jesus, it was his understanding of what was important in life and his understanding of the scripture that helped him counter the temptation even when the tempter had tried to use the scripture to tempt Jesus. Without understanding, Jesus would have lost his peace of mind pondering on the words of the serpent and in the end, he would have sinned.

Matthew 4:1-10 - KJV

1.   Then was Jesus led up of the Spirit into the wilderness to be tempted of the devil.
2.   And when he had fasted forty days and forty nights, he was afterward an hungred.
3.   And when the tempter came to him, he said, If thou be the Son of God, command that these stones be made bread.
4.   But he answered and said, It is written, Man shall not live by bread alone, but by every word that proceedeth out of the mouth of God.
5.   Then the devil taketh him up into the holy city, and setteth him on a pinnacle of the temple,
6.   And saith unto him, If thou be the Son of God, cast thyself down: for it is written, He shall give his angels charge concerning thee: and in their hands they shall bear thee up, lest at any time thou dash thy foot against a stone.
7.   Jesus said unto him, It is written again, Thou shalt not tempt the Lord thy God.
8.   Again, the devil taketh him up into an exceeding high mountain, and sheweth him all the kingdoms of the world, and the glory of them;

9.   And saith unto him, All these things will I give thee, if thou wilt fall down and worship me. 10.   Then saith Jesus unto him, Get thee hence, Satan: for it is written, Thou shalt worship the Lord thy God, and him only shalt thou serve.

Every temptation that causes man to sin and do something unrighteous, follows this pattern. It tries to use fear to take away one's peace then make them desperate enough to commit unrighteous acts.

Another example to consider is a case of someone who engages in crime to gain financial wealth. We know that the person is doing this for the pride and opulence that the financial wealth brings with it.

But before they get to this stage, they must have lost their peace of mind.

Firstly, such a person is involved with what might seem like a harmless interaction with either self or others. This conversation would be about their financial state, mostly about things they would like to have but can't have.

Then the conversation takes a turn and becomes one that forces him/her to wrestle with their conscience/moral. At this stage a person is forced to question how far they are willing to go to get the money, do they keep their process clean or accept to introduce some criminalities.

The next stage is the most critical because this is where fear is introduced. In this case, it is the fear of remaining poor/not having money as quickly as one would like. The fear is that if one doesn't get such a level of wealth, they have no real worth or respect in society. If such an individual is overtaken by this fear of missing out on such a level of luxury and societal status, the person will lose his/her peace of mind then the person will fall for the temptation to do anything to acquire the pride of wealth and luxury (feeling that his/her life will become peaceful again once they acquire these things).

If only they understand what is important in life (like Jesus did), and they understand that they are spirit beings created in the image of God (therefore cant be defined by earthly possessions), they wouldn't lose their peace over financial status thus wouldn't be desperate enough to engage in financial crime.

One common example is the temptation that pushes a person to commit fornication for the first time.

The first step is usually a seemingly harmless conversation either within one's self or with other people. The conversation could be about love, maturity, puberty, age or a wide range of topics that can lead to the next stage.

The second stage is about having sex in itself and the moral implications. At this stage one's conscience steps in while another voice challenges the conscience. This other voice could still be in one's head but inspired by an earlier interaction with a person or a form of misleading media. However, this seed was sown into the mind, the aim is to try and question the moral argument by one's conscience.

But the temptation doesn't work without the next phase which is the phase where fear is introduced. At this third phase, a person is made to view losing his/her virginity as an achievement that shouldn't be missed. The fear that if he/she is still a virgin then they are not viewed as mature or they would not be respected amongst their peers. In some cases, some ladies are made to fear that if they choose to stay virgins they will lose out on guys or a particular guy that they may have feelings for. This is where an individual either stands or falls. If he/she succumbs to the fear, and lose their peace of mind over the issue, they will fall for the desire to achieve the proposed pride of losing his/her virginity.

The moment they buy into the idea that losing their virginity would be a thing of pride, they lose their peace of mind till they have sinned.

One of the tricks of the devil is that this is a vicious circle. The devil will keep using this fear and lack of peace to keep pushing the person into unrighteousness. In the case of fornication, the devil will return with the lie that if one is not having constant sex, then they are missing out on life. And when he can get them to be having constant fornication, he can return with another lie that if it is only done with one partner, then that person is missing out. The next lie can be that fornicating with protection is for lame people. Then it can be about the kind of fornication engaged in. all the time using lies and fear to constantly trouble people's minds keeping them in a state of constant lack of peace.

This is why it is hard for people who engage in financial crime to stop. There is always a new target (for wealth and opulence) that the devil will use to take away the person's peace of mind so that they keep going back to crime.

Here you can see the relationship between peace and righteousness. Peace is like a shield for righteousness. Once peace is taken away, righteousness becomes exposed and weak.

If many people have understood this relationship between peace and righteousness, they would have been saved from a long spell of unrighteousness. I say this because many people stuck around situations that killed their peace of mind for so long and this drove them into a life of unrighteousness. If they had known, they would have gotten out of those situations that killed their peace as early as possible.

These situations could be work arraignments, abusive relationships, family ties, friendships and many other forms of entanglements. These relationships usually make people feel bad about themselves and constantly troubled in their minds. Filling their hearts with one type of fear and insecurity or the other. In the end, they lose their peace and become susceptible to unrighteousness. This is usually how a lot of addictions started (by staying around things and people that kill your peace). It could be as simple as a friend who always picks on you and tries to make you feel inadequate in one way or the other. It could be someone you have feelings for or even family members. It could be a social media handle or a celebrity you look up to. You need to pay attention to how you feel after engaging with that person or thing. If it takes away your peace and leaves your mind troubled, then it will make you sin sooner or later.

But this is not the only way to look at the relationship between peace and righteousness. Righteousness can also be seen as a stepping stone to peace. The more righteous a person is, the more peace of mind they should have. The two are co-dependent on one another.

Proverb 28:1 -KJV

1. The wicked flee when no man pursueth: but the righteous are bold as a lion.

David in the bible also seems to think that righteousness and peace go hand in hand

Psalms 119:165 - KJV

165. Great peace have they which love thy law: and nothing shall offend them.

Here David argues that those who are righteous will have great peace because they wouldn't get offended easily. How is this possible?

The answer is in the word understanding. The ability to be righteous and the ability to not get offended by things (especially people) are both rooted in the level of understanding a person has.

We have discussed earlier that the reason why many people do unrighteous things is down to fear and ignorance. If you have this understanding, you wouldn't get offended when people treat you in an unrighteous manner. You will have sympathy for their ignorance and fear rather than you getting offended. God himself demonstrated this in the story of Jonah.

This is the story of Nineveh. A city that God was thinking about destroying because of their evil ways. So, he sent Jonah to warn them. After running from his assignment, Jonah finally goes to Nineveh and warns them that they have offended God and are in line for destruction. The city rallied around and cried to God for forgiveness and God forgave them. But this made Jonah upset thinking God just wasted his time sending him to Nineveh. Jonah wanted them to be punished for their iniquities so bad because if they don't get punished, he would look like a false prophet who prophesied doom and it never happened. So, God decided to teach Jonah a lesson.

God provided a plant as shade for Jonah to rest under as he (Jonah) watched Nineveh from afar waiting for the moment it will be destroyed. When Jonah realised it would not be destroyed, he was angry with God and then God sent a worm in the night to eat up the plant that he was using as a shade.

Jonah got angry with God asking him why he had chosen to destroy a plant that did not offend him. But God's response was amazing.

God asked Jonah that if Jonah can have compassion on one plant, why can't he understand God having compassion on a whole city who as God described Them, don't know their right from their left.

Nineveh was a very successful city but was sinful. Despite their success in their physical endeavours, God still saw them as ignorant because of their evil deeds. In other words, if they had understanding, they would have been living right.

Jonah 4:6-11 - KJV

6.   And the LORD God prepared a gourd, and made it to come up over Jonah, that it might be a shadow over his head, to deliver him from his grief. So Jonah was exceeding glad of the gourd.

7.   But God prepared a worm when the morning rose the next day, and it smote the gourd that it withered.

8.   And it came to pass, when the sun did arise, that God prepared a vehement east wind; and the sun beat upon the head of Jonah, that he fainted, and wished in himself to die, and said, It is better for me to die than to live.

9.   And God said to Jonah, Doest thou well to be angry for the gourd? And he said, I do well to be angry, even unto death.

10.   Then said the LORD, Thou hast had pity on the gourd, for the which thou hast not laboured, neither madest it grow; which came up in a night, and perished in a night:

And should not I spare Nineveh, that great city, wherein are more than sixscore thousand persons that cannot discern between their right hand and their left hand; and also much cattle?

Therefore, ignorance is the real reason for all the evil going on in the world. It is the reason for evil deeds and the reason for our gross lack of peace both for those who do evil and those who take offence.

Thus, the take-home from this chapter is that both righteousness and peace are dependent on the level of understanding that a person has.

The more understanding a person has, the less likely the person is to be fazed by anything. Also, lack of understanding means ignorance and ignorance is a breeding ground for fear. The less a person knows and understands, the more fearful they are likely to be. And fear is an ingredient of temptation and unrighteousness no wonder the bible says ignorance is the reason why people perish.

Hosea 4:6 - KJV

6. **My people are destroyed for lack of knowledge:** *because thou hast rejected knowledge, I will also reject thee, that thou shalt be no priest to me: seeing thou hast forgotten the law of thy God, I will also forget thy children.*

Our next chapter is to see how Joy fits into this equation of the kingdom of God being righteousness, peace, and joy.

JOY

Romans 14:17 - KJV

17. For the kingdom of God is not meat and drink; but righteousness, and peace, and joy in the Holy Ghost.

We have established that the kingdom/character/life of God consists of righteousness, peace, and joy. We have been able to see the relationship between righteousness and peace, how there are codependent on one another. Now we need to examine the role that Joy plays in the kingdom/character/life of God.

To do this properly, we first need to understand Joy as a concept.

According to the dictionary, joy can be defined as a feeling of great happiness. but the truth is that Joy is a very difficult thing to define or describe. It isn't happiness that is why it is described as great happiness by the dictionary.

There are telling differences between happiness and Joy. Happiness is defined as a feeling of pleasure. But we can't really say for certain that Joy has anything to do with pleasure.

Let me tabularize the telling differences between happiness and Joy.

HAPPINESS	JOY
Happiness is a response of pleasure to an event or an action. This means that happiness is triggered by something external of a person.	Joy comes from within an individual, it isn't a response but a state of being.
It is temporary (short term), based on outward circumstances.	It can be long lasting based on inward circumstances
Expressed outwardly	Identified by inward peace and contentment

From the differences I have highlighted, it is easy to tell that happiness is something that belongs to the flesh. It is more like a stimulus reaction to things that we find pleasant. But Joy is something that is associated with the inner man (the spirit). It is not a reaction to anything but more of a byproduct of a way of life (moral way of life).

There are places in the bible that help us realise that Joy is a thing of the spirit. Joy is more of a conscious choice than a reaction.

1 Thessalonians 1:6 - KJV

And ye became followers of us, and of the Lord, having received the word in much affliction, with joy of the Holy Ghost:

Romans 14:17 - KJV

17. For the kingdom of God is not meat and drink; but righteousness, and peace, and joy in the Holy Ghost.

Just like righteousness and peace, joy is a thing that originates from inside and isn't triggered by circumstances.

But despite all the inconclusions on how to best describe Joy, I would say there is one word that best does the job; and that is satisfaction.

So, I would define joy as a state of satisfaction. A state of being satisfied irrespective of physical circumstances and happenings.

If this is true, then the kingdom/life/character of God is a life of righteousness, peace, and satisfaction.

This is a claim supported by David.

Psalms 17:15 - KJV

15. As for me, I will behold thy face in righteousness: I shall be satisfied, when I awake, with thy likeness.

In this verse, David seems to be describing what it feels like to exist in the likeness of God. And he calls it satisfaction. But the most intriguing thing of this verse is that he highlights righteousness as a prerequisite to this feeling or as a codependent attribute to satisfaction.

Social scientists believe that humans can't find satisfaction. Maybe they are right because according to David, satisfaction is something that you can only find when you operate with the likeness/character/life/kingdom of God.

But how is this so?

Firstly, we have shown that to operate with the kingdom of God is to operate by the holy ghost (inner man/spirit) and this will result in not fulfilling the lust and desires of the flesh. We also have seen that everything that can cause us to not be satisfied in life is all hidden in the desires and expectations of the flesh.

Galatians 5:16 - KJV

16.   This I say then, Walk in the Spirit, and ye shall not fulfil the lust of the flesh.

This lust of the flesh that makes us hungry for physical pleasures, recognitions and possessions are the basic things that fuel the dissatisfaction in our hearts. Thus, walking in the spirit through righteousness and peace will aid us in overcoming the lust of the flesh and help us experience Joy (satisfaction) in life no matter our physical situations or conditions.

Secondly, both righteousness and peace are rooted in understanding, therefore if Joy is a codependent element of the kingdom of God, therefore understanding is a key ingredient for Joy (satisfaction).

The basic reason why many people become dissatisfied in life is because of their lack of understanding.

If people understood that they are spirit beings and not their flesh, they wouldn't get dissatisfied by things that the flesh lust after. They would realise that physical wealth doesn't define who you are nor does physical appearance. If people had understanding, they would realise that physical pleasures can give you happiness which is momentary but can't give you peace and joy in your soul. The craze for sexual pleasures in this day and age is simply down to a lack of understanding. Some people even get so dissatisfied with their life because they feel they are not getting enough sex because they do not understand how insignificant it is. They do not realise that what their soul is craving for are peace and joy but sex can only entertain the flesh and give you happiness for a moment before they are back to feeling empty again due to the lack of joy(satisfaction) in their life.

The connection between righteousness, peace, and joy is understanding.

Another way to look at the relationship between righteousness, peace, and joy is that just like peace is protection to righteousness, joy is protection to peace and righteousness. This means that when a person gets to a place of joy, the devil will need to get rid of his/her joy before he takes away his/her peace of mind then gets him/her to do something unrighteous.

Let's look at the temptation of Eve. The first thing the serpent did was to get her to not be satisfied with her life, thereby getting rid of her joy. He did this by making her feel that there is more than what she is. That the way she was wasn't good enough so she would need to eat of the fruit of the tree of knowledge of good and evil.

Genesis 3:4-5 - KJV

4.   And the serpent said unto the woman, Ye shall not surely die:

5.   For God doth know that in the day ye eat thereof, then your eyes shall be opened, and ye shall be as gods, knowing good and evil.

What would have saved Eve would have been her satisfaction with how God made her (this would have kept her joy) and would have protected her peace. The moment she became dissatisfied with who she was (therefore losing her joy), her peace of mind became exposed and the moment she let herself think about it she lost her peace of mind. And when the peace of mind was gone, it became easy for her to do something unrighteous by disobeying God.

Genesis 3:1-7 - KJV

1.   Now the serpent was more subtle than any beast of the field which the LORD God had made. And he said unto the woman, Yea, hath God said, Ye shall not eat of every tree of the garden?
2.   And the woman said unto the serpent, We may eat of the fruit of the trees of the garden:
3.   But of the fruit of the tree which is in the midst of the garden, God hath said, Ye shall not eat of it, neither shall ye touch it, lest ye die.
4.   And the serpent said unto the woman, Ye shall not surely die:
5.   For God doth know that in the day ye eat thereof, then your eyes shall be opened, and ye shall be as gods, knowing good and evil.
6.   And when the woman saw that the tree was good for food, and that it was pleasant to the eyes, and a tree to be desired to make one wise, she took of the fruit thereof, and did eat, and gave also unto her husband with her; and he did eat.
7.   And the eyes of them both were opened, and they knew that they were naked; and they sewed fig leaves together, and made themselves aprons.

This shows that joy (satisfaction in life) is a necessity if we are to protect our peace of mind and then our righteousness.

In the case of joseph in Potiphar's house, Joseph was saved foremost because he was satisfied with whatever his master was giving him. He must have understood that he wasn't defined by anything physical or his position as a servant. If he wasn't satisfied with life, sleeping with his master's wife would have come across as an opportunity. Potiphar's wife was making her advances day after day but if he wasn't satisfied with what he was given, he would have given her advances more thought and it would have taken away his peace of mind.

He was just a housekeeper but he did it with diligence and gratitude and joy(satisfaction).

Genesis 39:1-10 - KJV

1. And Joseph was brought down to Egypt; and Potiphar, an officer of Pharaoh, captain of the guard, an Egyptian, bought him of the hands of the Ishmeelites, which had brought him down thither.

2. And the LORD was with Joseph, and he was a prosperous man; and he was in the house of his master the Egyptian.

3. And his master saw that the LORD was with him, and that the LORD made all that he did to prosper in his hand.

4. And Joseph found grace in his sight, and he served him: and he made him overseer over his house, and all that he had he put into his hand.

5. And it came to pass from the time that he had made him overseer in his house, and over all that he had, that the LORD blessed the Egyptian's house for Joseph's sake; and the blessing of the LORD was upon all that he had in the house, and in the field.

6.   And he left all that he had in Joseph's hand; and he knew not ought he had, save the bread which he did eat.   And Joseph was a goodly person, and well favoured.

7.   And it came to pass after these things, that his master's wife cast her eyes upon Joseph; and she said, Lie with me.

8.   But he refused, and said unto his master's wife, Behold, my master wotteth not what is with me in the house, and he hath committed all that he hath to my hand;

9.   There is none greater in this house than I; neither hath he kept back any thing from me but thee, because thou art his wife: how then can I do this great wickedness, and sin against God?

10.   And it came to pass, as she spake to Joseph day by day, that he hearkened not unto her, to lie by her, or to be with her.

Even Jesus was satisfied with whatever he had and who he was, that was why when the devil tried to get him to fall by promising the riches of this world, he didn't fall.

The question now becomes, if what is required to keep one's joy is to stay satisfied does this mean that we are not meant to have ambitions in life? How then are we supposed to find motivation in life?

The answer to this is in one word 'purpose'. And we shall discuss how this will help us stay satisfied and yet motivated in life. And ultimately protect our peace and righteousness.

PURPOSE

If an individual wants to constantly experience joy no matter what his/her situation or condition is, he/she must always find a way to stay satisfied. But how can a person stay satisfied even when things are not looking good?

How is a person expected to be motivated in life if he/she is expected to stay satisfied/contented at all times?

The answer to this is purpose. Man must live a life of purpose if he/she is to stay satisfied no matter what.

Purpose is defined as the reason for which something is done or created or exists.

Everything in life has a purpose, be it a nonliving or living thing. This includes man.

When a person isn't living for a purpose they are living for pride/lust. This pride/lust is the reason why a person will develop selfish expectations that prevent one from being satisfied.

In life, every action taken is done for either of two reasons. Pride or purpose.

You buy a car either for purpose or for pride.

You wear a dress either for purpose or for pride.

You get a degree either for purpose or for pride.

You marry a spouse either for purpose or for the pride of getting married or getting married to that particular person.

every cause of action taken in life is done either for purpose or pride.

Everything made, is made either for purpose or pride. Everything in life is subject to this principle (including man).

We can find the purpose for which God made man in Genesis chapter 1, first in verse 26 and then after creating man in verse 27 God explains his purpose for creating man by giving him instructions on what he is expected to do on the earth in verse 28.

Genesis 1:26-28 - KJV

26. And God said, Let us make man in our image, after our likeness: and let them have dominion over the fish of the sea, and over the fowl of the air, and over the cattle, and over all the earth, and over every creeping thing that creepeth upon the earth.

27.   So God created man in his own image, in the image of God created he him; male and female created he them.

28.   And God blessed them, and God said unto them, Be fruitful, and multiply, and replenish the earth, and subdue it: and have dominion over the fish of the sea, and over the fowl of the air, and over every living thing that moveth upon the earth.

Before verse 26, God had instructed the Waters and the Earth to bring forth creatures after their kind, and they did bring forth the fish of the sea, and the fowls of the air, and other living things that moveth upon the earth. So, in verse 26, God was simply sharing his plans with the Waters and the Earth of making a superior being that would overlook every other creature.

In verse 27 he creates man in his image, and in verse 28 he explains man's purpose to man. But in verse 28 he breaks it down into four parts. The first two are to be fruitful and to multiply, and the last two are to replenish the earth and to subdue the earth.

Before we analyse the four aspects of man's purpose, I would like to point out that the first two are the foundation for the existence of all living things. No living creature should violate these two. This is evident in the fact that in verse 22 God also instructed other living things to be fruitful and multiply.

Genesis 1:22 - KJV

*22.   And God blessed them, saying, **Be fruitful, and multiply,** and fill the waters in the seas, and let fowl multiply in the earth.*

Be fruitful

This paints the picture that all living creatures are expected to be like trees and bare fruits. One very important thing to note is that trees don't bear fruits for their benefit but the benefit of other creatures. Therefore, God's first instruction to man is that he must bear fruits that other people and creatures can benefit from. That is man's primary purpose.

The word fruitful means to produce useful and helpful results. Thus, God's primary assignment for man is that man must be useful and helpful. Man must be a blessing in one way or another to other people and creatures. This is man's fundamental purpose.

Therefore, if a person wants to live a life of purpose, then he/she must have a mindset of usefulness. Such a person's motivation would be to be useful. In other words, to be productive.

There is usually a thin line between living a life of purpose and living a life of pride. For example, person A wakes up in the morning to go to work because he wants to make money, and the money buys him some material things and some recognition. Person B wakes up in the morning to go to the same work but with a different mindset. Person B is looking forward to being productive and putting a smile on the face of the customers.

Person A is motivated by pride, while person B is motivated by purpose. The consequence is that person A is more likely to commit a crime or do evil in his work than person B. Person A is more likely to succumb to lying and scheming and cheating just to get more money or get to the top of his/her career while person B is less likely to fall for temptations on the job. The difference between the two of them is that one is motivated by purpose (being useful), the other is motivated by pride. Person A will always live a life of dissatisfaction because his measurement of accomplishment is tied to acquiring material things for selfish reasons. And until he gets those things, there is no satisfaction. And if he/she gets those things he/she lusts for, he will just create new targets and lusts to go after which will leave him/her constantly dissatisfied and lacking joy. But person B will stay satisfied as long as he/she wakes up to constantly put in the effort to be useful and be a blessing irrespective of what he or she is doing or maybe going through.

To live a life of purpose, a person's mind must be tuned to finding pleasure and honour in being useful rather than finding pleasure and honour in the pride of life. If your mind is tuned towards one, it cannot be turned towards the other.

To this end we can say that if Eve's motivation was tuned towards being useful in the garden, she would have gone about fulfilling her purpose of being useful, she would have found reason to be pleased with herself and thus she wouldn't have been motivated by the pride of becoming a god. Also, if she had applied herself to be useful, she would have discovered amazing things about herself that would have shown her how much she is like the almighty God.

Genesis 3:5 - KJV

5. For God doth know that in the day ye eat thereof, then your eyes shall be opened, and ye shall be as gods, knowing good and evil.

In the case of Joseph, it was clear that he was more interested in being fruitful in whatever he was doing than chasing after pride/lust. This is why he was satisfied with himself even though he was just a housekeeper.

Genesis 39:3-6 - KJV

3. And his master saw that the LORD was with him, and that the LORD made all that he did to prosper in his hand.

4. And Joseph found grace in his sight, and he served him: and he made him overseer over his house, and all that he had he put into his hand.

5. And it came to pass from the time that he had made him overseer in his house, and over all that he had, that the LORD blessed the Egyptian's house for Joseph's sake; and the blessing of the LORD was upon all that he had in the house, and in the field.

6. And he left all that he had in Joseph's hand; and he knew not ought he had, save the bread which he did eat. And Joseph was a goodly person, and well favoured.

He still adopted this approach even when he was elevated to being the right-hand man of Pharaoh. He was more concerned about being fruitful than chasing after pride.

Genesis 41:46-49 - KJV

46. And Joseph was thirty years old when he stood before Pharaoh king of Egypt. And Joseph went out from the presence of Pharaoh, and went throughout all the land of Egypt.

47. And in the seven plenteous years the earth brought forth by handfuls.

48. And he gathered up all the food of the seven years, which were in the land of Egypt, and laid up the food in the cities: the food of the field, which was round about every city, laid he up in the same.

49. And Joseph gathered corn as the sand of the sea, very much, until he left numbering; for it was without number.

Jesus too was also more interested in his ministry of being a source of salvation to the souls of many than acquiring the riches of this world for himself, this is why he was satisfied enough not to fall for the temptation he faced.

Multiply

Multiplying is the second basic assignment or purpose given to all living creatures. To multiply means to reproduce. This is the second most important thing to any creature thus it should be the second most important source of motivation for every creature.

If this is the second most important source of honour and joy, it is the second thing on the list we must strive to excel at.

Multiplying doesn't just mean reproducing it also means taking good care of what we reproduce (our offspring). This is the second most important task of a person, to reproduce and take good care of our offspring (to be good parents). If this is done right, we then can derive pleasure and honour from the wellbeing of our offspring. This includes both physical and spiritual wellbeing. It is not just a responsibility to multiply physically but to also multiply knowledge and understanding to the younger generation. By offspring I do not mean only biological, this refers to everyone we come across who is of the next generation and need our guidance and care.

Unfortunately, many people are so distracted by their pursuit of the pride of life to the point where they neglect this second most important assignment. Many people are so preoccupied with their chase for wealth, recognition, physical gratifications that they neglect their responsibilities to their offspring. This is how much living for pride can affect our purpose. Many parents think it's all about money so all they throw at their children is money. No mentorship or mental care. Most times this is because they are more interested in chasing after the pride of life thus, they can't fulfil their purpose to their children.

The second most important thing that a person should find pleasure and honour in, is to be beneficial to their children and the younger generation. This is what multiplying entails. If you are not focused on deriving honour from this purpose, you will leave a vacuum to feel worthless and this will open you up to fear and the pursuit of more pride.

Replenishing the earth.

This third instruction given to man is given to him to prevent him from destroying the earth. What God was saying to man is that he is the one to manage the earth. Whatever you take from it as you live here, you must replenish. A practical example is how man cuts down trees and kills wildlife without any management plan that replenishes these things. We just keep taking from nature without putting back (replenishing) what we take.

But if we take a look at the world we live in today, man has not been able to fulfil his assignment of replenishing the earth because man is busy chasing after pride. We are always looking for more wealth, more comfort, more recognition through owning more properties. We don't seem to know when to stop and replenish what we have taken from the earth. And in all our greed for more, it is the earth that has to supply the resources to meet our greed.

If only we would live out our true assignment (purpose) by being more kind to the earth but our pursuit of pride is in the way of this. If we are focused on replenishing the earth, it will reduce the appeal for the pride of life that we have. Thus, being concerned about our environment can also help us constantly be in a mindset that makes it difficult for pride to sneak in.

Subdue the earth

This is the final part of God's instruction to man when he created man. This is the part where God lets man know that he is in charge of the earth and the proceedings on the earth. Man has the power to make use of the earth to suit his needs.

In other words, man is the boss of things in the physical, nothing that comes from the earth is more valuable than man.

But because of our pursuit for the pride of life, we have disregarded this instruction in many ways. Today we seem to value so many things more than we value one another. In our selfish individual pursuits for pride, we disregard and disrespect other people. We value material possessions and social status more than our fellow men. We even take lives just to acquire pride.

Anybody who lives a life of purpose will always realise the value of other people and would never place anything above his fellow man. This is possible because if you live a life of purpose, you would have realised your value and this will enable you to realise the value in others. Just like we said in our previous chapter, no one can love others if they don't first have self-love. This is because of the principle that no one can give what they don't have. Thus, if a person has not recognised his/her value, they can't see value in other people. And if a person places value in the pride of life, he/she can't place value in his/herself. Thus, they can't place value on others.

Living a life of purpose will help you recognise your place as a man (created in the image of God), as one created to subdue the earth. This will also enable you to see the same in other people. If Eve was living a life of purpose, she would have seen herself in this light as well as her husband. She wouldn't have fallen nor would she have dragged her husband with her because she would have also seen him in this light (a man created in the image of God).

One other way to analyse the choice of pride or purpose is that when God gave man his purpose in Genesis 1:28, man was still a spirit without flesh. Thus, man's purpose is engraved in his spirit. This means that living a life of purpose is living according to one's spirit. The flesh was given to man as a tool to execute these instructions(purpose). Thus, living a life of purpose is to be led by the spirit while a life of pride means one is led by his flesh. This means the tool (the flesh) has now become the master (of the spirit).

Even the gifts that are given to us as individuals are given to us to fulfil our assignments(purpose) here on earth. Whatever your natural, God-given gift or talent is, it is given for you to use in being fruitful, multiplying, replenishing the earth and subduing it. It is not given to us to become rich or famous or to gather material things for ourselves. Riches could be a consequence of fulfilling purpose but if one never gets the riches of this world, it is still possible to stay satisfied and full of joy if they are motivated by purpose. They will derive honour from their daily effort to be a blessing to anyone they come in contact with

Everyman who discovers the things God has deposited in him will have to make the choice of using it for purpose or pride. This is the temptation that Jesus faced.

Jesus had finished praying and fasting and was now ready to begin his ministry. He would have just discovered how much understanding and knowledge and power he had in him. Just at that very moment, the tempter came to tempt him.

What many did not realise was that the tempter was simply trying to make Jesus choose a life of pride over a life of purpose. Jesus could have used his power to turn the stone into bread for himself or could have chosen to go the way of the tempter and become very rich. With the power and knowledge, he had, he definitely could have gone after riches and gotten it with ease. But Jesus rejected the offer thereby rejecting a life of pride for a life of purpose.

Matthew 4:1-10 - KJV

11.   Then was Jesus led up of the Spirit into the wilderness to be tempted of the devil.

12.   And when he had fasted forty days and forty nights, he was afterward an hungred.

13.   And when the tempter came to him, he said, If thou be the Son of God, command that these stones be made bread.

14.   But he answered and said, It is written, Man shall not live by bread alone, but by every word that proceedeth out of the mouth of God.

15.   *Then the devil taketh him up into the holy city, and setteth him on a pinnacle of the temple,*

16.   *And saith unto him, If thou be the Son of God, cast thyself down: for it is written, He shall give his angels charge concerning thee: and in their hands they shall bear thee up, lest at any time thou dash thy foot against a stone.*

17.   *Jesus said unto him, It is written again, Thou shalt not tempt the Lord thy God.*

18.   *Again, the devil taketh him up into an exceeding high mountain, and sheweth him all the kingdoms of the world, and the glory of them;*

19.   *And saith unto him, All these things will I give thee, if thou wilt fall down and worship me.*

20.   *Then saith Jesus unto him, Get thee hence, Satan: for it is written, Thou shalt worship the Lord thy God, and him only shalt thou serve.*

Jesus chose to derive his honour, and joy from living a life of purpose than deriving honour and joy from material and earthly things (pride).

This made Jesus stay satisfied and contented. This in turn will protect the joy in his spirit, which in turn will protect his peace of mind and ultimately his righteousness.

Unfortunately, many people just live for physical achievements, qualifications, recognitions, possessions, etc. which means that they can never be satisfied because there will always be more achievements, recognitions, attentions, possessions, etc. to chase after. But living for purpose means that you get to evaluate yourself based on your effort to be a blessing to others. And as long as you always make the effort, you will always be satisfied/pleased and contented with yourself.

There is an easy way to do all this without trying too hard, and that way is called love.

LOVE

It seems like tedious work trying to maintain the kingdom of God in you and keeping the holy ghost functional and operational at all times. This is because you have to protect your joy, your peace and your righteousness from the devil.

But there is an easy way out of struggling to stay righteous, protect your peace and remain joyful. This way is called love.

The kingdom/character/life of God is righteousness, peace, and joy. But there is also one place in the bible that uses one word to describe who God is.

1 John 4:8 - KJV

8. He that loveth not knoweth not God; for God is **love.**

If the summary of God's personality is love, then the summary of the kingdom/character/life of God is love. Which means love covers righteousness, peace, and joy. Love is the kingdom of God. Love is the character of the holy ghost (the inner man). If God is love and we are created in the image of God, then our original character is that of love, it is who we truly are. Thus, anytime we are not living this way, we are malfunctioning (we are sinning).

The bible clearly shows that love covers righteousness.

Romans 13:8-10 - KJV

8.   *Owe no man any thing, but to love one another: for he that loveth another hath fulfilled the law.*

9.   *For this, Thou shalt not commit adultery, Thou shalt not kill, Thou shalt not steal, Thou shalt not bear false witness, Thou shalt not covet; and if there be any other commandment, it is briefly comprehended in this saying, namely, Thou shalt love thy neighbour as thyself.*

10.   *Love worketh no ill to his neighbour: therefore **love is the fulfilling of the law.***

Here we see that love will help you fulfil all the laws of God.

Another way to look at it is that love is the greatest commandment that exists.

In the book of Mathew in chapter 22, Jesus was asked what he thought the greatest commandment was and his response was love.

Matthew 22:35-40 - KJV

35.   Then one of them, which was a lawyer, asked him a question, tempting him, and saying,

36.   Master, which is the great commandment in the law?

*37.   Jesus said unto him, Thou shalt **love** the Lord thy God with all thy heart, and with all thy soul, and with all thy mind.   38. This is the first and great commandment.*

*39.   And the second is like unto it, Thou shalt **love** thy neighbour as thyself.*

40.   On these two commandments hang all the law and the prophets.

Jesus said that the greatest commandment was to love God. But he goes further by saying that the next law he was about to mention is the same thing as the first which means they mean the same thing. The second law he was talking about was to "love thy neighbour as thyself".

There are also other verses in the bible that agree with this assertion that loving one's neighbour is the same as loving God.

1 John 4:20-21 - KJV

20.   If a man say, I love God, and hateth his brother, he is a liar: for he that loveth not his brother whom he hath seen, how can he love God whom he hath not seen?

21.   And this commandment have we from him, **That he who loveth God love his brother also.**

Here John supports the statement that one cannot love God without loving others.

The other story that shows that the only way to love God is by loving your neighbours is in Mathew chapter 25.

Matthew 25:34-46 - KJV

34.   Then shall the King say unto them on his right hand, Come, ye blessed of my Father, inherit the kingdom prepared for you from the foundation of the world:

35.   For I was an hungred, and ye gave me meat: I was thirsty, and ye gave me drink: I was a stranger, and ye took me in:

36.   Naked, and ye clothed me: I was sick, and ye visited me: I was in prison, and ye came unto me.

37.   Then shall the righteous answer him, saying, Lord, when saw we thee an hungred, and fed thee? or thirsty, and gave thee drink?

38.   When saw we thee a stranger, and took thee in? or naked, and clothed thee?

39.   Or when saw we thee sick, or in prison, and came unto thee?

40.   And the King shall answer and say unto them, Verily I say unto you, Inasmuch as ye have done it unto one of the least of these my brethren, ye have done it unto me.

41.   Then shall he say also unto them on the left hand, Depart from me, ye cursed, into everlasting fire, prepared for the devil and his angels:

42.   For I was an hungred, and ye gave me no meat: I was thirsty, and ye gave me no drink:

43.   I was a stranger, and ye took me not in: naked, and ye clothed me not: sick, and in prison, and ye visited me not.

44.   Then shall they also answer him, saying, Lord, when saw we thee an hungred, or athirst, or a stranger, or naked, or sick, or in prison, and did not minister unto thee?

45.   Then shall he answer them, saying, Verily I say unto you, Inasmuch as ye did it not to one of the least of these, ye did it not to me.

46. And these shall go away into everlasting punishment: but the righteous into life eternal.

Here Jesus was simply saying that the way to love God is by loving others.

But if we go back to Mathew 22:39 Jesus adds a clause that makes things interesting. Jesus says "love thy neighbour **as thyself**". This is because no one can love others if he/she doesn't love his/herself. This is bound by the principle that no one can give what they don't have.

To put Mathew 22:35-40 in perspective, Jesus was simply saying that to love God you must love your neighbour, and to love your neighbour, you must love yourself. Therefore, to love God, you must love yourself.

The most intriguing part is in verse 40 where Jesus says that every other law is subject to this law. Thus, every law is under the law that one must love his/her self.

This means that if one can love his/her self, and others they will fulfil all the commandments of God.

The author of the book of Romans also shares this understanding.

Romans 13:8-10 - KJV

11. Owe no man any thing, but to love one another: for he that loveth another hath fulfilled the law.

12. For this, Thou shalt not commit adultery, Thou shalt not kill, Thou shalt not steal, Thou shalt not bear false witness, Thou shalt not covet; and if there be any other commandment, it is briefly comprehended in this saying, namely, Thou shalt love thy neighbour as thyself.

*13. Love worketh no ill to his neighbour: therefore **love is the fulfilling of the law.***

If you take a look at the ten commandments, you would see that all the commandments were given for the benefit of the people and not God's benefit. People have failed to realise that the laws and commandments of God are for our benefit.

For example, the law of "thou shall not lie" is for our benefit. Lying doesn't do any damage to God but it does damage to the liar. It is the liar that needs to wrestle with his conscience thereby losing his peace. The lair still will need other lies to cover the first lie and in the long run, will lose trust from other people.

Thou shall not kill, is a law to preserve both one's soul/mind/heart and the lives of others. We can't kill God; thus, this law is for our benefit.

Thou shall not commit adultery, is a law to protect one's marriage, and one's home. These days you can add avoiding sexually transmitted diseases to the list of the benefits of this law. God is not at risk of such diseases; it is you and I that are at risk. So, such a law isn't for God's benefit but ours.

Neither shalt thou bear false witness against thy neighbour is a law given to protect the person who is being accused falsely and the integrity of the individual who thinks of being a false witness. What does God benefit here? Nothing.

Neither shalt thou desire thy neighbour's wife, neither shalt thou covet thy neighbour's house, his field, or his manservant, or his maidservant, his ox, or his ass, or anything that is thy neighbour's. This law is to our benefit because covetousness will take away our inner peace and could also take away the peace between us and our neighbour.

Even the law of the sabbath given to the Jews was not for God's benefit but their benefit. They were slaves in Egypt and thus never knew how to rest because all they did in Egypt was to labour so Moses gave them the sabbath to help them rest and recharge mentally and spiritually. This is why when Jesus was accused of dishonouring the sabbath, he asked them who was made for who? Was man made for the sabbath or the sabbath for man? In other words, the sabbath was instituted for man to use for man's benefit thus the sabbath can't be lord over the man.

Mark 2:27-28 - KJV

27.   And he said unto them, The sabbath was made for man, and not man for the sabbath:

28.   Therefore the Son of man is Lord also of the sabbath.

Ordinarily, if you love yourself, you should take out time to rest from daily physical work. You should find time to grow spiritually by seeking knowledge and understanding from God. This is what the law of the sabbath was all about; loving one's self.

Even the law against worshipping other gods and idols wasn't given because God felt threatened or so, it was given for our own sake. We are created in the image of God; how then should we bring down ourselves to be beneath another thing labelled as a god. God just wanted us not to lose perception of who we are.

The point here is that all the commandments given by God are for our good and protection, therefore loving one's self and others is a way to effortlessly fulfil the commandments of God.

Galatians 5:14 - KJV

14.   For all the law is fulfilled in one word, even in this; Thou shalt love thy neighbour as thyself.

In summary, if Eve had kept her love for herself, she wouldn't have disobeyed God by eating the fruit of the tree of knowledge of good and evil (she wouldn't have desired to be like the gods), and also if she had kept her love for others, she wouldn't have given her husband to eat with her. But like we said earlier no one can give what they don't have, thus before you can love others, you would have to love yourself. In the same vein, Eve did not show love for herself when she ate from the tree of knowledge of good and evil, she can't show love to her husband by preventing him from eating it too.

There is another passage of the bible that shows that love is the gateway to righteousness, peace, and joy.

1 Corinthians 13:1-8 - KJV

1.   Though I speak with the tongues of men and of angels, and have not charity, I am become as sounding brass, or a tinkling cymbal.

2.   And though I have the gift of prophecy, and understand all mysteries, and all knowledge; and though I have all faith, so that I could remove mountains, and have not charity, I am nothing.

3.   And though I bestow all my goods to feed the poor, and though I give my body to be burned, and have not charity, it profiteth me nothing.

4.   Charity suffereth long, and is kind; charity envieth not; charity vaunteth not itself, is not puffed up,

5.   Doth not behave itself unseemly, seeketh not her own, is not easily provoked, thinketh no evil;

6.   Rejoiceth not in iniquity, but rejoiceth in the truth;

7.   Beareth all things, believeth all things, hopeth all things, endureth all things.

8.   Charity never faileth: but whether there be prophecies, they shall fail; whether there be tongues, they shall cease; whether there be knowledge, it shall vanish away.

In this passage, love is replaced with the word charity. The writer starts by saying that no matter how religious a person is if you do not have a heart of love, you are nothing. This is true considering that God is love.

This writer also goes further to describe what love is and how it functions.

From verse 4, we begin to see how love can help protect one's joy love suffereth long means that no matter what an individual is going through, if they have a heart of love, they can stay strong. Love does not envy, doesn't accommodate pride (charity vaunteth not itself, is not puffed up). Love seeketh not her own shows that it doesn't accommodate selfishness. By avoiding envy, pride, and selfishness, a person is more likely to live a life of purpose and stay satisfied thereby protecting their joy.

An individual can't even live a life of purpose (in service to others) if that individual doesn't have love inside of him/her. It is as simple as that.

Love is not easily provoked shows that a person who walks in love is will always have peace of mind.

Love "thinketh no evil; rejoiceth not in iniquity" highlight the relationship between walking in love and walking in righteousness.

Love "rejoiceth in the truth" shows that a person who walks in love will always seek to know the truth thus will get knowledge and understanding. And we know that understanding is a foundation for righteousness, peace, and joy.

Choosing to walk in love for one's self and others is truly a life hack. This is why Jesus summarized all the commandments into love.

Matthew 22:35-40 - KJV

38.   Then one of them, which was a lawyer, asked him a question, tempting him, and saying,

39.   Master, which is the great commandment in the law?

*40.   Jesus said unto him, Thou shalt **love** the Lord thy God with all thy heart, and with all thy soul, and with all thy mind.   38. This is the first and great commandment.*

*41.   And the second is like unto it, Thou shalt **love** thy neighbour as thyself.*

42.   On these two commandments hang all the law and the prophets.

Let's be honest, it takes self-love for one to find satisfaction even when life's conditions are not favourable. And it takes love for others to overcome covetousness that can also kill satisfaction and contentment. It truly takes love to find peace and joy. This means it takes love to walk in the spirit (holy ghost).

The book of Galatians agrees to the above by summarizing the fruit (manifestation of the spirit) as love, peace and joy.

Galatians 5:22-23 - KJV

22.   But the fruit of the Spirit is love, joy, peace, longsuffering, gentleness, goodness, faith,

23.   Meekness, temperance: against such there is no law.

Notice how the fruits of the spirit share similarities with what the author of Romans describes as the kingdom/nature of God. How the fruit of the spirit contains peace and joy, and the rest can be summarised as righteousness. Also notice how it all starts with love.

Indeed, love is a gateway to the kingdom of God (righteousness, peace, and joy). And since the kingdom of God is in the holy ghost, therefore love is the gateway to manifesting the holy ghost.

SUMMARY

The summary here is that to live a life of righteousness, peace, and joy, one just needs to live a life of love.

The big question now is why do people find it so hard to love themselves and therefore others?

The answer is ignorance.

People are simply ignorant of who we are and how we are in the image of God. This has made many people measure themselves in the likeness of the flesh and its, flaws, lusts, pride, and dissatisfaction. This has made it hard for people to fall in love with themselves.

People are unaware that the kingdom of God (righteousness, peace, and joy) are already gifted by God to our inner man (the holy ghost). Many are even ignorant that the holy ghost is the same as our inner man/spirit; the real us. So, they are looking for its manifestations outside of them, meanwhile, they are walking around with the capacity to manifest the holy ghost (righteousness, peace, and joy).

People are ignorant that living a life of purpose is a good way to awaken the joy deposited inside the spirit by God. It is also a good way to see the amazing side of one's self and fall in love with one's self.

People are ignorant that choosing to live a life of love for one's self and others is a straightforward way to be like God and manifest his kingdom thereby experiencing righteousness, peace, and joy.

Plainly put, people are ignorant about their ignorance. This is why people perish.

Hosea 4:6 - KJV

6. My people are destroyed for lack of knowledge: because thou hast rejected knowledge, I will also reject thee, that thou shalt be no priest to me: seeing thou hast forgotten the law of thy God, I will also forget thy children.

This is why the bible says that the ultimate thing an individual need in life is understanding.

Proverb 4:7 - KJV

7.   Wisdom is the principal thing; therefore get wisdom: and with all thy getting get understanding.

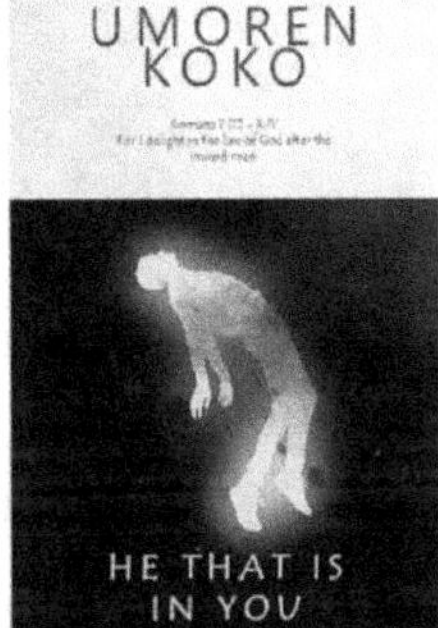

THE FREEDOM SERIES

This is a series of five
books designed to
free
your soul from the
control of the flesh
and the mindset of

sin.

Umoren Koko is a life coach, a teacher and an economist born in the city of Lagos in Nigeria. He has a first degree in Economics from Covenant University in Nigeria. He also has a Masters Degree in International Business And Management from Nottingham Trent University.
Motivated by the quest to understand life with the aim of helping people live a much simpler and fulfilling life, Koko has spent most of his adult years seeking to understand God and his ways so that he can be a medium for educating people on the things of God and Life.

This is the fourth book of the freedom series; a series of five books designed to make your soul free from the control of the flesh and the mindset of sin.

RIGHTEOUSNESS, PEACE, & JOY.